Colours Of My Heart

Melanie Wilding

BookLeaf Publishing

Presentation by *BookLeaf Publishing*

Web: www.bookleafpub.com

E-mail: info@bookleafpub.com

ISBN: 9789357616850

First edition 2022

When?

When?
When will the dam break?
When will the words that are tumbling, floating,
tripping, poking
Wanting to be witnessed, discovered
Spill forth?
When will the arrow be released from the
quivering bow?
When will the caged birds be set free?
When will the stories of my heart liberate me?
Tales wander through the halls of my soul
Lost
Seeking the door

Free

2

The shackles that bound you have fallen
You are the flower that has been choked by the
weed
But you could not be vanquished
The spell has broken, his power faded to nothing
Awaken your dormant spirit
The fire within still flickers
Step out from the shadows of fear
Your scars do not define you
Reclaim your lions heart
And rise from the ashes like a phoenix!

Liberation tastes sweet
The wind is beneath your wings
Float, glide, soar, trip the light fantastic!
Glorious is she who revels in her wildness
You cannot be tamed
Leap into the great unknown
Let your dreams lead you astray
They are your heart's desire
Possibilities run riot
Live, for you are free

Forsaken

Where has my mind gone?
Do not forsake me!
Don't leave me here
Lost and alone
People seem malevolent in this labyrinth
Strange faces looming out of the fog
To haunt my waking nightmare
Memories confused and misused
Clarity slipping like sand through the hourglass
Time is running out
Faster and faster, until the person I was will
vanish
Leaving behind an empty shell
All light gone from the windows to my departed
soul

The mysterious man had come again
Love shining like the brightest star in a velvet
sky
Who was this Romeo that declared undying
affection?
Sadness emanated from him as realisation hit
I knew him not
Why did he linger so? I was not his Juliet
Chords of a song floated softly through the air

With a jolt, knowledge pierced the madness
My beloved! My sweetheart!
Familiarity was mine and so was he
Our hearts entwined for all eternity
I would find him in another lifetime
Silence fell upon our world
And the spell was broken

Mayhem erupted
The chaos of my dreaded reality taking over
completely
Insanity at the helm in a sea of turmoil
Disappearing in the wildness of a demented
mind
All was lost

A Moment

5

I told you it was okay to go
Trying to be brave
The quaver in my voice gave me away
You smiled and tucked my hair behind my ear
The love in your eyes
Was nearly my undoing
You may be gone, but your spirit lives within me
Wild and free

Lightning Strike

I believe in the lightning strike
The bow from Cupid's arrow
That pierces the unsuspecting lonely heart
Serendipitous encounters that fate surely
conspired to create
Smouldering eyes meeting through the crowd
As though no one else existed

Butterflies fluttering, swirling, dancing
Gazing in wondrous joy at the world, smitten
For your bliss turns everything to gold
Colours brighter, music all the more beautiful
On earth, but not of it
As you float on cloud nine

A pounding heart that cannot slow
Lips trembling with anticipation
Chemistry that ignites, burns, consumes
Passion unbridled
The surrendering of one soul to another
Two hearts beating as one
I believe in love

Lost Boy

A lost boy wanders alone
In the gathering dark
Unseen and unheard
He goes where he fears to tread
Adrift on despair
Suffering buried so deep
No one can hear him scream

Forces beyond his control
Conspiring and conniving
To desecrate and corrupt
Until all innocence departed

The sins of the father
Like bullet holes in his soul
The sins of the mother
Eyes willfully blind
Washing her hands, but the blood will forever
remain
Stained black on his heart

The scars have a heartbeat
Pulses of pain rewiring the brain
Creating an encompassing oppression
Twisted and tormented

Abandoned in a waking nightmare of reining
horrors
A circle of violence
Imprinted on a troubled mind

A crushed boy; a broken semblance of a man
Simmering behind oceans of stormy blue
A seething, writhing rage consumes
Lives lay scattered like leaves in his wake
His own shattered beyond repair
Spiraling down the depths of depravity
A prisoner of his own device
Bandaid solutions for a straitjacket mess
Nothing and no one can heal

From the ashes of hurts
Betrayed; defeated; trapped
Another identity rises
The lost boy a mere wisp in the shadows
Powerless against such reckless hate
He cowers; so alone
All hopes of resurrection fading

Surrounded by the dregs of society
Fans the flames of fury
He has no home, he has no future
Nothing to lose

A Love Letter To A Dream

Wherefore art thou, my lover in dreams?
The Prince Charming who enter's unbidden in
many thoughts; waking or dreaming
A welcome interloper
If you are but a fantasy, then let me linger in this
mystical fairytale ever more
You traverse amongst my heart's desires
Haunting and tormenting
I wait with restless longing, and I despair
But the vision of hope that is you, sustains me
Close my eyes
Make a wish
May my words cast the spell to weave you into
being

A knight in shining armour brought to life
Conjured from the vivid imaginations of
weavers of epic tales
Proof I'm not the only believer
You awaken the butterflies in my stomach; a
thousand wings fluttering madly
My breath, tremulous; the very air is you
All senses ignited, delighted
Pulse racing out of time to the rhythm of you
Eyes ablaze, you gaze upon me

Burning, yearning
And I am consumed

The world fades to white noise
There is only us
Souls entwined in a cosmic dance
Destiny and fate collided
A love that transcends space and time
I open my eyes
Ecstasy tattooed across my heart
Only to crash to earth
How can I love a figment of my imagination?

Disillusioned

Despondent, disheartened
Your careless indifference like a sword
Piercing through armour, touching my heart like
a feather stroke
It was enough
Melancholy has unfurled it's dark wings
Like an eclipse, turning everything from light to
shadow
Shades of black colours the world

Disappointment and love seem intertwined
Weariness goes soul deep
You are but one; my Lothario
About to be scattered to the wind
Left behind in my trail of broken romances
Clinging to me like cobwebs

Still waters run deep
Behind hazel eyes
But you will never know the depths
The ripples are disappearing
As are you, like you never were
The surface cool and calm once more
Belying what lies beneath

Self Sabotage

It hides in the shadows
Lurks on the edge of your consciousness
Haunting your footsteps
Like a stalker, waiting to strike

Commanding, dominating, enslaving
One step forward, two steps back
A vicious dance
Dreams lie in glittering pieces
After the savage thrust of the self sabotage knife

Homesick

I am homesick for places I've never been, and
places I have
Wanderlust infuses my very being
Gives flight to my restless feet
Distant and near shores beckon
Like a beacon to a lost ship on lonely waters
Searching for home
Somewhere to belong

I am homesick for bygone days I cannot get
back
Moments that were but fleeting
Left their imprint until this heart stops beating
Memories precious, yet bittersweet
Romanticised by the passage of time
Take on a rosy glow none can tarnish

I am homesick for a time before my own
Idolised in my eyes
To escape feeling like an outcast
An alternate reality
Inspiring, electrifying, expressive
That speaks to my soul

I am homesick for the stars

For the ones I have lost that reside there
Their stardust twinkling, guiding
Watching; waiting
My eyes travel ever upwards
Seeking; beseeching
Dreams bring them from the heavens
A double edged sword of devotion and sorrow
Grief carried, the price of love
Bleeding through the cracks that loss created
Until we meet again

Villain

In some stories, you will always be the villain
Vilified, no regard for truth that isn't distorted
Ensnared in a web created by their narrow mind
The high horse clung to so rigidly, so
imperiously
Is made of glass
Cracks, they do creep

Paint me as the villain
Whatever gets you through the night
But you sure as hell ain't no hero!
True colours will emerge
Over the passage of time

Temporary Love

Eyes meet
A suggestion of sensuality
Unspoken promises tickle senses
Images begin to play
Temperatures rise

Fingers intertwined
Lips touch, burn
Desire runs high
Melting into each other
In the hush of the midnight hour
Shadows in the light of the moon
Witnessing passions unrestrained
Soaring into ecstasy

A momentary encounter
Shooting stars colliding
An explosion of sparks
A brilliant supernova
Before passing into the night
Never to meet again

Butchered

A devastating diagnosis
A solution promised
Urgency felt, for you to grasp this lifeline
One question, one answer, the tipping point
"If this was your mother, would you tell her to
do it"
"Yes"

A long operation ensued
Cut from ear to ear
The remaining scar the least of your reminders
You never were the same again

Part of your soul was lost that day
Your life irretrievably altered
Which in the end
Was all for nothing

Hours were spent in front of mirrors
A stranger looking back
Scrutinising, agonising
A wreck you didn't want to see
But couldn't look away from

Quality of life, all but erased

Simple joys taken away
A grotesque mockery of a mouth
Is what they left behind
Filled with metal
Deformed, mutilated

The anguish and suffering
Betrayed by your eyes
Hard to witness, to bear
Butchered, there is no other word
For what they did to you

Grief

It is love persevering
With nowhere to go
Welling up until it overflows
A tide that comes and goes
You know not when

Waves crashing upon your shore
Sometimes nearly drowning
Other times floating
Hanging on for dear life
Until it recedes

Situations, places, where it's imminent
Or, an unexpected sucker punch to the heart
A testament to love deeply felt
Scar tissue tenderly forms at your core
Evidence of healing, of strength
A thing of beauty, for those who see

Ballad Of My Heart

Music is a part of my soul
Essential as breathing
Melodies beat through my heart
Lyrics serenade my mind
Vocal chords sing tunes
Rhythms compel hands to tap, feet to dance

Powerful enough to move me, groove me
Goosebumps shiver over my flesh
Heartstrings are strummed, stroked, plucked
The reverberations vibrating, echoing
Across my being

A time traveling portal
Transporting instantly to moments frozen in time
Songs for each significant memory
Arouse emotions

Unfailingly everlasting
Rising in crescendo
A harmonious love affair
The perfect accompaniment to me

Overthinking

The bane of my existence
Trapping me in webs of what if's
Different scenarios creating chaos
Stealing joy
Breaking my own heart

And yet
This fertile mind has a plethora of ideas
Waiting to be discovered amongst the clutter
My imagination leaps and bounds
When set free

Head In A Book

Opening up the covers
Words rise up, luring me in
Falling into the pages
I make my escape

Across the expanse of white
Between the swirls of ink
I plunge into the depths
Immersed in the magic I grip in my hands

Traversing other's imaginations
Intermingled with my own
I wander, entranced
Living a thousand lives

Loneliness

23

Loneliness strikes like a viper
Tendrils spreading through veins
Until it spirals and twines around your heart
Crushing it with a cold intensity

A lonely little island adrift on the sea of
humanity
Perceived by a melancholic mind
Falling into an abyss of isolation
Despairing of the sun to chase away the shadows

Little One

In the fertile darkness you blossomed quietly
Life was finding it's way
My unsuspecting mind missed small cues
But you were not meant for this world

A bombshell revelation
Before I had a chance to grasp the knowledge of
your existence
A brutally blunt statement, so casually declared
Ripped that apart
Your life was slipping away before my eyes

Utterly stunned, silent tears fell
How could I not know?
Instant blame I placed upon my shoulders
Expected to move on, as if you never existed
An untold story to carry
The insensitivity of others pierced my already
aching heart

You never knew fear, and you were never alone
In the warmth of my womb that cradled you
When I think of you, little one
I wonder what you would've been
A lingering what if, imprinted in my being

Exposed

25

The introvert part recoils in horror
I shiver, as if touched by cold
Silent screams echo through me
An overwhelming desire to hide
When sharing my words

Exposed fragments of my soul
Glittering in the glare of spotlights
Innermost thoughts
Few are privy to know
But for the love of expression
I endure the pain
Of feeling stripped bare

Paul

I never will forget the way your head dropped
Unable to break the devastation we already
knew
The love of your life by your side
Bravely voicing the horror you couldn't

In those all too short days
Your spirit and humour prevailed over the
hovering darkness
Precious memories made
The nightmare nearly forgotten
Love conquering almost all

I never will forget your shaking hands
As you fought the pain you kept quiet
Cancer appearing from the shadows, to grab you
in it's malignant clutches
The rising fear propelling me
Pleading for aid, pleading for you

That long corridor full of strange faces
An audience to your torment
Uncontrollable convulsions wracking your body
My choked vocal chords, unable to scream for
help
Shock and anguish wrapped around my throat

I never will forget your slurred voice
Expressing your wish to go home
It broke me, it breaks me still
Final goodbyes
Could you hear them?

Your racing heart slowing
A sighing final breath
Your pupils dilating, as your soul left
The nurses wordless confirmation
Silence hung heavy

I never will forget walking to your coffin, feet
dragging
Touching your cold forehead with a shaking
hand
A smile on your lips
Looking for all the world that you lay dreaming

Watching your shrouded body being lowered
into the ground
Feeling the dirt sifting through my fingers
Dropping it on your grave
Dad's hand on my shoulder, as he shakily
whispered your name
The gargoyle we placed by your marker amongst
the flowers
I never will forget you, my little brother

9 789357 616850